# God is Stretching Me

*From a Season of Stretching to a Lifetime*

**Melanie Lane**

© 2025 Melanie Lane. All Rights Reserved.
To God be the glory for the words written in this book. This work is the result of prayer, faith, and divine inspiration. It is dedicated to the healing and encouragement of others through the power of God's Word and personal testimony.

No part of this publication may be reproduced, distributed, or transmitted in any form or by any means—electronic, mechanical, photocopying, recording, or otherwise—without the prior written permission of the author, except in the case of brief quotations embodied in critical articles, reviews, or teachings, provided proper credit is given.

Scripture quotations are taken from the Holy Bible, New King James Version® (NKJV), copyright © 1982 by Thomas Nelson. Used by permission. All rights reserved. Other translations are noted where applicable.

This book is a work of nonfiction. Some names and identifying details may have been changed to protect the privacy of individuals. The testimonies shared reflect the author's true experiences and the faithfulness of God in every season.

For permissions, speaking engagements, or ministry inquiries, please contact:
Melanie Lane
Email: **mlane@thestretchcircle.com**

Published in the United States of America.
First Edition, 2025

# Dedication

*To my beautiful children — Xavier, Xzyia, and Joshua —*
*You are my why, my joy, and my living testimonies.*
Each of you were born during seasons of uncertainty, yet through every trial, God revealed His purpose in the pain and His promise in every push.
To Zakaiden (KJ) — you came to us in a sacred season of stretching, and your presence is proof that grace still flows in the middle of the stretch. This book belongs to you as much as it does to me.
**With all my love,**
**Mommy**

*But now, O LORD, You are our Father;*
*We are the clay, and You our potter:*
*And all we are the work of Your hand.*
                              Isaiah 64:8

# From a Season of Stretching to a Lifetime

Welcome to My Stretch.
*This is not just a book—it's a journey.*

## Min. Melanie Lane

# Table of Contents

**Dedication** .................................................................3

**"Being confident of this very thing, that He who has begun a good work in you will complete it until the day of Jesus Christ." — Philippians 1:6 (NKJV)**...................................................................11

**Introduction: What is Stretching?**.........................12

**Chapter One: A Shaky Start, A Strong Foundation** .................................................................................14

**Chapter Two: From Brokenness to Breakthrough** .................................................................................19

**Chapter Three: Stretched by Fire – 2018 and the Turning Point** ..........................................................25

**Chapter Four: God in the Gaps – The Single Mother's Strength**......................................................31

**Chapter Five: Released to Rise** .............................41

**Chapter Six: The Stretch Doesn't End on the Mountain**................................................................44

**Stretch Declarations**................................................53

**Scripture Meditation Page** ......................................53

# Acknowledgments

**To God be the glory**—the One who carried me when I could not carry myself.

To every person who watched me stumble but also saw me rise again—**thank you**. Your silent support and watchful grace did not go unnoticed.

To my Pastor, Prayer Warriors, Mentors, and those who interceded for me during battles no one else saw—**your faith became my fuel**.

To my mom, my dad's (I miss you both), my Auntie Mattie, and Cristashia—you walked with me when the path was uncertain.
To Sharmanita and Valery—you surrounded me with love and always knew how to speak a word in season.

To my spiritual mother, Ruby—thank you for always believing in me and standing by as you watched both me and my children blossom.

Felicia, you already know. Lashonda and Anthony, thank you.

To every **single mother**, every **struggling woman**, every **person walking through a stretching season**—this book was written with you in mind. *You are not alone.* God sees you. He is stretching you, not to break you, but to bless you.

With heartfelt gratitude, I thank **Ruby Garrison** and **Loretta Fergerson**—two anointed women of God whose prayerful hearts and gifted hands helped bring this book to life. Your wisdom, encouragement, and excellence have been a blessing beyond measure. May the Lord continue to multiply all you do for His Kingdom.

**Stretching isn't punishment, it's preparation.**

*Melanie*

# Dear Reader,

First, thank you.
Thank you for picking up this book. Thank you for trusting me with your time, your heart, and your own stretch journey.

I didn't set out to write a perfect story. I set out to tell the real one.
The story of what it feels like to be stretched beyond what you thought you could handle — and to discover that even there, God is holding you together.

This book was written in the middle of tears, prayers, disappointments, and unexpected victories. It was birthed out of seasons where the only thing stronger than my struggles was the God who carried me through them.

Maybe you're in a stretch season right now.
Maybe you feel tired, unseen, uncertain, or even broken.
If so, I want you to know this — **you are not being punished. You are being prepared.**

Every stretch is a sign that God isn't finished with you.
Every tear is a seed being watered for your future harvest.
Every delay, disappointment, and detour still carries purpose in His hands.

As you read these pages, my prayer is that you find more than just my story.
I pray you find pieces of your own story tucked within — and more importantly, that you find hope, strength, and an

unshakable reminder that the stretch is real...
**but our God is more real.**

This journey is sacred ground, and I am honored to walk it with you.

Keep stretching.
Keep believing.
Keep trusting that the God who began the good work in you will be faithful to complete it.

In His Stretching Love,
**Melanie Lane**


*"The stretch is real, but so is the victory."*

"Being confident of this very thing, that He who has begun a good work in you will complete it until the day of Jesus Christ."
— Philippians 1:6 (NKJV)

# Introduction: What is Stretching?

Stretching is uncomfortable.

It pulls at your limits. It tests your strength. It exposes places you didn't know needed healing, reshaping, or surrender. And yet, as painful as it may be, stretching is not the same as breaking.

I didn't know this truth when my journey began. I thought I was just trying to survive. I didn't see the hand of God in the chaos. I didn't understand how deep the work He was doing in me would go.

In 2016, my life shifted. Not suddenly, but significantly.

At that time, I was a single mother of three children—each in a different stage of life. My oldest son had just gone off to college on a full scholarship. My daughter was preparing to walk the stage for her high school diploma. And my youngest, my baby boy, was still navigating elementary school. On paper, that might sound manageable. But let me tell you the truth: I was working a full-time job in Human Resources, picking up part-time hours at a home goods store in the evenings and some weekends, and grinding through full-time graduate studies.

There were nights I cried myself to sleep, praying over bills, begging for energy, wondering if I was failing my children and myself. There were days when I didn't even have enough gas in the car, and I had to choose between groceries and school supplies. There were moments when I questioned if God even heard me anymore.

But He did.

This book is my story, my stretch, my valleys and my small victories. It's a testimony of how God doesn't just show up in the breakthrough—He's present in the breakdown, too.

I wasn't proud of how my motherhood began. I had three children, by three different men, none of whom stood by me long-term. And the shame of that lingered. But grace found me. Grace lifted me. Grace taught me how to raise my children not in the shadow of my mistakes, but in the light of God's mercy. Today, they are God-fearing individuals who love the Lord, not because I was perfect, but because I was stretched—and I chose to stretch toward Him.

I want you to know that if you're being stretched right now—by grief, disappointment, financial strain, heartbreak, or just the weariness of life—you're not alone. And you're not being punished. You're being prepared.

This is not just a season. For some of us, stretching becomes a lifestyle. But that's not something to dread. That's something to embrace—because it means God is still molding you, still working on your behalf, and still guiding you toward your mountain.

In the chapters ahead, I'll share moments of raw honesty, deep pain, and undeniable hope. I'll open the door to my past and show you how scripture became my anchor when I was sinking. And more than anything, I pray that these words stretch you too—into healing, into trust, and into believing that God still has a plan for your life.

Let's begin this journey together.

—**Melanie Lane**

# Chapter One: A Shaky Start, A Strong Foundation

*"God doesn't need a perfect beginning to build an unstoppable future."*

I never imagined my story would begin like this. Pregnant. Alone. Ashamed. Not once, but three times.

I was a single mother of three children, each with a different father. It's a truth that used to make me hang my head in guilt. Not because I didn't love my children—because I did with everything in me—but because I feared what others would think. I feared what *God* thought. I thought I had failed Him, failed myself, and failed the dreams I once held as a little girl imagining what motherhood would look like.

But isn't it just like God to build something solid from something society calls shaky?

What the world labeled a mistake; God saw as ministry in the making.

In the midst of my mess, I made a choice: to raise my children on **biblical principles**. I knew I couldn't give them a picture-perfect home, but I could give them the Word of God. I could teach them how to pray. I could speak life into them. I could model strength in weakness and teach them that our circumstances do not define our worth—God does.

And while doing all of that, I kept pressing forward with my education.

In **2007**, I graduated with a **Bachelor of Science in Resource Management**.
By **2008**, I fast-tracked and completed my **Master's in Human Resources**.
Not long after, I pursued and completed another **Master's in Leadership and Management**.
And now, in **2025**, I'm currently pursuing a **Bachelor of Arts in Biblical Studies**—because my heart and calling are fully invested in knowing and rightly dividing the Word of God.

Every degree, every class, every late-night study session—it all happened in the stretch. I was a full-time mom, full-time worker, and full-time student, all while trusting a full-time God.

**"There is therefore now no condemnation to those who are in Christ Jesus…" (Romans 8:1)**

I held onto that scripture like a lifeline. Because the enemy tried to convince me that my past disqualified me from a future. But grace said otherwise. Grace said *keep going*. Grace said *you're still chosen*.

By the time 2017 rolled around, my children were growing into their own paths—each at a different stage of life. My oldest son had just left for college on a full scholarship (a moment I still weep over with gratitude). My daughter was in her junior year of high school, full of dreams and drive. And my baby boy was still navigating elementary school with all the joy and energy only the youngest can bring. But he was not a fan of school at all.

And me? I was running on fumes.

I was working **full-time as a Human Resources Representative**, **part-time as a customer service rep** at a local home goods store and **attending graduate school full-time**. I'd leave the house before sunrise, juggle meetings and assignments between shifts, and return home to help with homework, cook dinner, or going from one practice to another and manage household responsibilities. Some days, I didn't even remember driving home. My body was moving, but my soul was crying out.

I was being stretched—and at the time, I didn't even know what that meant.

What I did know was that I was tired. Mentally. Physically. Emotionally. Spiritually. But somehow, God kept me.

**"He gives strength to the weary and increases the power of the weak." (Isaiah 40:29)**

I lived that verse. When I thought I had nothing left, He would breathe just enough strength into me to get through the day. He didn't always remove the load, but He carried me through it. And slowly, I began to understand something deeper—that stretching was not punishment. It was preparation.

My life wasn't neat or polished, but it was honest. It was rooted in faith. And though my start was shaky, my foundation was being built on something immovable—on Someone who never let go of me even when I let go of myself.

I taught my kids how to tithe with one dollar and how to trust God for five loaves. I showed them how to praise in lack and rejoice in small victories. We cried together. We prayed together. We survived together. And through it all, I kept hearing God whisper:

**"You are not broken. You are becoming."**

This chapter of my life was not just about surviving hard seasons. It was about discovering that God does His best work in the stretch. But even with a stronger foundation, life didn't stop stretching me. In fact, the next season would take me deeper than I ever expected—into a breaking point that would become a breakthrough.

*Let's step into that part of the story together...*

---

**Reflection Questions:**

1. Have you ever felt like your past disqualified you from your future?
2. What does Romans 8:1 say to that lie?
3. In what areas of your life do you feel stretched right now?
4. How might God be using that stretch for your strengthening?

**Prayer:**
**Lord, thank You for the grace that covers my past, strength that carries my present, and purpose that awaits my future. Help me to stand on Your Word when life feels overwhelming. Let my shaky places become sacred places where You show up and stretch me into who You've called me to be. In Jesus' name, Amen.**

"But little did I know, the biggest test of my faith and motherhood was still ahead — when brokenness would meet breakthrough."

## LESSONS FROM THE STRETCH

- God can build strength from shaky beginnings.
- Grace covers what guilt tries to condemn.
- Our circumstances do not define our worth — God does.
- Faithfulness in small things leads to great victories.
- God uses our stretch seasons to deepen our foundation, not destroy it.

# Chapter Two: From Brokenness to Breakthrough

*"The cracks in your heart are where God's glory shines through the brightest."*

There's a kind of brokenness that doesn't come with bruises. It comes in waves—in silent tears behind closed doors, in exhaustion that feels endless, in disappointments that stack higher than your faith feels.

I've lived in that kind of brokenness.

There were moments in my life where I felt like I was losing more than I was gaining. Friendships faded. Opportunities slipped away. Sometimes, it wasn't even betrayal that broke me—it was the silence. It was showing up for others who didn't show up for me. It was being surrounded by people and still feeling unseen.

I was a mother, a provider, a student, a co-worker, a sister, a friend, a churchgoer… and somewhere in all that noise, I began to wonder if anyone saw *me*. Not the version of me that was always holding it together. The real me—the tired me. The "God, I don't know how much more of this I can take" me.

I knew what it felt like to lay in bed with a smile on your face for your children and a hole in your heart for yourself.

I was grieving things I never gave myself permission to mourn. Missed opportunities. Failed relationships. The family I dreamed of that didn't look like the one I had. And yet, every morning, I had to rise as if everything was okay, because three little hearts were depending on me to be their safe place.

And that's when I learned one of life's hardest lessons: **you can be broken and still be a blessing**.

**"To all who mourn in Israel, He will give a crown of beauty for ashes, a joyous blessing instead of mourning…" (Isaiah 61:3)**

That verse became an anchor for me. I would whisper it when I didn't feel beautiful. When life felt more like ashes than joy. I held onto the promise that if I stayed faithful, God would turn my mourning into ministry.

Somewhere in my pressing, a breakthrough was forming. Not the kind that changes your circumstances overnight—but the kind that transforms you *from the inside out*. My faith began to deepen—not because things got easier, but because I had no choice but to depend on God in every area of my life.

There were weeks when I didn't know how bills would get paid, but somehow, they did. There were times I walked into church feeling empty, but I left full because of one word, one hug, one scripture. There were moments I prayed not just with words, but with groans—desperate for God to just *see* me. And He did.

**"My grace is sufficient for you, for my power is made perfect in weakness." (2 Corinthians 12:9)**

Looking back now, I see that my breakthrough didn't happen in one day—it happened in layers. It happened when I stopped performing and started **surrendering**. It happened when I let go of people who were draining me and made space for God to pour into me. It happened when I stopped looking for healing in others and found it in His Word.

I had to forgive people who never said sorry. I had to release bitterness that had made a home in my heart. I had to believe that even in my brokenness, I was still chosen.

If you're in a season where it feels like your life is falling apart, let me remind you—God doesn't waste pain. He rebuilds with it.

This wasn't just about single motherhood or financial stress. It was about learning how to trust God when trusting Him didn't make sense. It was about watching Him make ways in the wilderness of my life. It was about letting Him carry me when I had no strength to walk.

Breakthrough didn't come when I "fixed" everything. It came when I finally said, "God, I can't do this alone." And He whispered back, "You never had to." The song "You are my Strength" became my daily national anthem. It was my song of praise.

## When the Storm Hit

An incident happened in 2017 that altered the course of my son Xavier's path. At the time, he was thriving at the university he attended on a full scholarship — a young man with promise, purpose, and a bright future ahead. I remember the moment vividly: I was driving to vacation Bible Study at my home church in Fort Deposit, when my phone rang. It was Xavier. His voice was shaky, hesitant. He didn't come right out and say what happened — but within minutes, the news broke. His name was all over the internet. My heart sank.

By the time I pulled into the church parking lot, the weight of the unknown pressed heavily on my chest. Sitting in VBS, I pulled up the article and began to read it. Shock. Fear. Disbelief. I could hardly process the words. Tears welled up in my eyes. I stood up, walked straight to my Pastor's office, and with trembling hands, passed him my phone. I could barely speak, but through the tears I managed to whisper, *"Why? He knows better."*

In that moment, the enemy tried to convince me it was over — that everything we had prayed, worked, and believed for was shattered beyond repair.
But **Jesus showed up**. Right on time — just like He always does. Even when the situation looked irredeemable, God was already working behind the scenes. He was in the midst of it all. He was stretching me deeper than I ever imagined, but He was also setting the stage for His glory to be revealed.

Miraculously, Xavier never spent a single day in jail. Court case after court case, my mother and I showed up — prayed up, standing firm — believing that the same God who opened the Red Sea could open a way for my son.
Every Hearing was another opportunity for me to trust. Another opportunity for me to worship through the tears. It was all part of my stretch. It was all part of my breakthrough.

I never gave up. I refused to let go of my faith. I continued to pray. I continued to worship my Lord and Savior. Because even when brokenness tries to tell us it's the end, God whispers, *"I'm not finished yet."*

**"The righteous cry out, and the Lord hears, and delivers them out of all their troubles."**
*— Psalm 34:17 (NKJV)*

What looked like devastation became deliverance.
What looked like a breakdown became a breakthrough.
Because when Jesus shows up — He shows out!

Breakthrough is rarely neat. It's messy, it's painful, and it often feels like walking through fire. And for me, the year 2018 would become a defining moment—a fire I didn't see coming, but one that would refine everything inside of me.

*The stretch was about to reach a whole new level.*

---

**Reflection Questions:**

1. What area of your life feels most broken right now?
2. What would it look like to surrender it to God?
3. Who or what are you still holding onto that may be blocking your breakthrough?
4. Can you identify a moment in your past where God turned your mourning into strength?

**Prayer:**
**Lord, I surrender my brokenness to You. Every disappointment, every hurt, every area I tried to fix on my own—I give it to You now. Show me how to trust You with the pieces and help me to see the beauty You are creating out of my ashes. For God, You are my strength, strength like no other. Thank You for being the God of my breakthrough. In Jesus' name, Amen.**

## LESSONS FROM THE STRETCH

- God can build strength from shaky beginnings.
- Grace covers what guilt tries to condemn.
- Our circumstances do not define our worth — God does.
- Faithfulness in small things leads to great victories.
- God uses our stretch seasons to deepen our foundation, not destroy it.
- True strength is found in dependency on God, not independence.

# Chapter Three: Stretched by Fire – 2018 and the Turning Point

*"Fire doesn't just destroy — in God's hands, it refines and defines."*

If I had to mark a turning point in my life—a year when everything began to change—it would be 2018.

By then, I was no stranger to the hustle. I had been balancing single motherhood, graduate school, a full-time HR job, and a part-time retail position. I knew what it meant to stretch my days and stretch my dollars. But in 2018, God began stretching *my faith* in a whole new way.

That year, I felt the pull.

Not just the pull of responsibilities or exhaustion—but a divine tug on my spirit. I didn't fully understand it then, but I now know God was calling me—calling me deeper, calling me higher, calling me into ministry.

And I wasn't ready.

Me? Ministry? I looked at my life and felt disqualified. My past. My pain. My imperfections. My plate was already overflowing, and I had nothing else to give. I told God, "Not now." But His silence wasn't absence—it was patience. And in His patience, He kept working on me.

**"Before I formed you in the womb I knew you, before you were born I set you apart; I appointed you as a prophet to the nations." (Jeremiah 1:5)**

That scripture used to make me nervous. But the more I wrestled with it, the more I realized: God doesn't wait for us to feel ready—He waits for us to say *yes*. Even in the middle of chaos, He was preparing me for purpose.

2018 also stretched me emotionally. My oldest son was a Junior in college on a full scholarship. My daughter was wrapping up high school, full of ambition and excitement. My youngest, my Babyboy, was still in elementary school—young, bright, and full of questions. Three children in three different seasons. And me? I was holding it together with nothing but faith, coffee, mountain dews and whispered prayers.

I was tired. Spiritually and physically. Yet God was not finished stretching me.

During that year, I began to lose relationships I once leaned on. People started fading from my life. Some left by circumstance. Some left by choice. And though it hurt, I began to understand that elevation requires separation. I couldn't take everyone with me into where God was leading me.

Something inside of me was shifting. I no longer had time for surface-level religion. I didn't want to just *go to church*—I wanted to *be the church*. I wanted to *know God*, not just know about Him. I began deep-diving into His Word. I started asking harder questions. I stopped playing church and started craving Kingdom.

Eventually, I made a difficult decision: to leave the church I had been attending. I wasn't running from offense—I was running toward revelation.

The stretch continued.

In 2019, I finally surrendered to the call and said *yes* to ministry. Then came **January 2020**, The start of the year I got **married**— a decision I felt I made in obedience, though the path was not smooth at all. It was a roller coaster. But even through the bumps and breakdowns, God never let go of me.

Then came a date I'll never forget: **August 9, 2020.**

It was the day I stood and delivered my **trial sermon**—publicly accepting the call God had placed on my life back in 2018. What made it even more special - It was my **Babyboy's birthday**. And the Holy Spirit had chosen that date for me to commit to doing God's will in ministry.

I don't believe in coincidences—only divine orchestration. That day was layered with meaning:

- **The 8th month—August—represents new beginnings.**
- **The 9th day—symbolic of completeness and birthing.**
- **My son's birthday—new life. My sermon day—new purpose.**

And the sermon God gave me to preach was **"God ALWAYS Wins"**
Text: *Luke 1:37 – "For with God nothing will be impossible."*

God wasn't just calling me to ministry—He was completing something in me.

**"Being confident of this very thing, that He who has begun a good work in you will perform it until the day of Jesus Christ." (Philippians 1:6)**

So much changed that year. But one thing stayed the same: I was still being stretched.

And now, I understood it.

Stretching wasn't a punishment. It was preparation. It was God molding me for the mountain—even while I was still in the valley. That was not just a message—it was my *mandate*. It was my *testimony*. Through all the heartbreak, exhaustion, and uncertainty, I had seen God's hand win every time. When it looked like I would lose my mind, God won. When I thought I had failed as a mother, God showed me I was more than enough. When doors closed, He opened better ones. God. Always. Wins.

That sermon was not just for the congregation—it was for me.

***When Love Hurts and Hope Hangs On***

In 2021, my world shifted once again when my husband was admitted into the hospital. That moment marked another life-altering season—one that brought waves of stress I could not have anticipated. I felt completely alone, even though I was surrounded by people. It was a different kind of loneliness, the kind that seeps into your spirit when the one you love seems unreachable.

He had always been strong-willed, even hardheaded at times, and he often chose the rougher path through life. That stubbornness, what some would call resilience—created a wall between us that was hard to tear down. We found ourselves navigating more than just his physical illnesses; we were facing emotional and spiritual roadblocks that threatened to divide us.

First came the leg amputation, followed by a vision correction procedure that went terribly wrong. As if that wasn't enough, he then underwent neck surgery. The journey took us from hospital rooms to rehab centers, back to the hospital again, and then back to rehab. It felt like a never-ending loop of hardship. Each phase drained me—physically, emotionally, spiritually.

I watched him become someone I had to care for. And in that caregiving, I found myself grieving—not just for his health, but for the relationship we used to have. The weight of being strong for everyone else while feeling unseen and unheard myself became another layer of the stretching God was allowing.

But even in the midst of this, I held on. To faith. To grace. To the quiet hope that God still had a plan for our story. It was rough and I really wanted to throw in the towel on this relationship.

But faith isn't built just on the mountaintop moments. It's forged in the everyday gaps—the places where need meets provision, heartbreak meets healing, and exhaustion meets unexpected strength.

*Come with me into the next chapter—where I learned how God shows up in the gaps.*

---

**Reflection Questions:**

1. Have you ever run from something God was calling you to do? What held you back?
2. What relationships or environments might God be asking you to release in this season of stretching?
3. Can you look back and recognize how a specific date or event was divinely aligned?

**Prayer:**
Lord, thank You for calling me even when I didn't feel ready. Thank You for stretching me through loss, growth, and divine shifts. Help me to trust Your timing, surrender to Your calling, and never run from the fire that purifies me. Let every part of my journey reveal Your glory. In Jesus' name, Amen.

## LESSONS FROM THE STRETCH

- God calls us in the middle of our chaos, not after it's cleaned up.
- Stretching seasons often lead to our divine assignments.
- Saying "yes" to God doesn't require perfection—only willingness.
- Separation is sometimes necessary for elevation.
- God completes what He begins, even when we feel unfinished.

# Chapter Four: God in the Gaps – The Single Mother's Strength

*"Where your strength ends, God's miracles begin."*

I didn't have everything I wanted, but God made sure I had everything I needed.

That's the story of my life as a single mother—stretching dollars, faith, and time. There were days when the gas tank was nearly empty, the fridge was close to bare, and my strength was on "E." But somehow, every time I reached the end of myself, God met me there—with provision, with peace, with power.

When people talk about miracles, they often think of the big ones: Red Sea moments, cancer disappearing, the blind seeing. But I've learned to see miracles in the small, quiet ways God shows up:

- A surprise check in the mail right when a bill was due.
- A co-worker dropping off a meal without knowing I hadn't eaten all day.
- A secondhand coat in my son's exact size in a donation pile.
- Waking up with just enough strength to do it all over again.

**"And my God will supply every need of yours according to His riches in glory in Christ Jesus." (Philippians 4:19)**

God filled in every gap. Emotionally, Spiritually, and Financially. When I didn't know how I was going to make it—He did.

After accepting my call into ministry and delivering my trial sermon in 2020, I expected everything to get easier. But instead, life taught me that *calling does not cancel challenge.* Ministry didn't eliminate my struggles—it redefined how I responded to them. I no longer panicked when the pressure came. I praised. I no longer begged—I believed. Because I had *seen* what God could do.

But the stretching didn't stop. It never really does.

As I leaned deeper into God's Word and walked out my faith, I found myself desiring more than just religious routine. I wanted truth. Transformation. I didn't have time for empty titles or fake friendships. I wanted to walk in Kingdom purpose, not just church attendance.

That desire led me to leave the church I was attending and come under **watch care** in a new ministry. That season was refreshing—it gave me a deeper understanding of the Word and what it meant to build a church on solid biblical principles. I was growing, and so was my daughter, Xzyia and son, Joshua. But deep down, I knew… **this wasn't the final stop.**

In **2023**, something shifted.

I came under watch care in a ministry that taught me the Kingdom of God and how to build on solid, biblical principles. That season sharpened my discernment and deepened my understanding. But even there, God whispered, *"This is not where you'll stay."*

On my way to church one Sunday morning, I noticed a small, newly established church along my usual route. I passed it week after week, noticing the sign out front with service times. It looked quiet, humble—but something about it stirred in my spirit.

Then it happened.

One rainy day after work, as I was driving home, I past that same church, the Holy Spirit spoke:
**"Go get your son and come back to Bible Study here at 6pm."**

It was so specific. So clear. So unexpected. But, I obeyed.

I picked up my son and said, "Baby, we're going to Bible Study." He looked at me and simply said, "Okay, Mommy."

We (Joshua and I) pulled up to the church. Only one car was there—and it was pulling off. I rolled my window down and so did the woman in the other car. It was the **First Lady**, and even in the rain, God made room for a divine connection. She shared the Bible study information with me, and from that day forward, **we stayed**.

That little church became home. Not just for me—but for my *Babyboy*. God planted us there. And I knew, without question, this is where God wanted me for this next stretch of the journey.

But nothing could prepare me for the storm that was coming next.

There are some years that take more than they give. Some seasons that don't ask for permission before turning your world upside down. For me, that year was an unrelenting stretch of grief, responsibility, heartbreak, and deep, desperate faith.

As a single mother, I was no stranger to pressure. I had become skilled at wearing many hats—provider, nurturer, counselor, chauffeur, chef, prayer warrior, and disciplinarian. My days were a balancing act. But that year, it was as if the weight of all the roles I carried grew heavier with every passing week. I wasn't just juggling—I was bleeding. Quietly. Faithfully. Determinedly.

I found myself constantly in hospitals. It became my second home. One week it was my mother. The next, my dad—my

Papa. Then my Auntie. I memorized the smell of antiseptic, the quiet hum of machines, the look in a nurse's eyes when she didn't know what to say. I smiled politely and held back tears as doctors delivered updates I didn't want to hear. I was holding everyone else together—but inside, I was unraveling.

And just when I thought the whirlwind might let up, I was blindsided by something I never saw coming: **my Babyboy was diagnosed with diabetes.**

He was young. So full of life. And now, hooked to IVs and confined to a hospital bed at **UAB Children's Hospital**, where we stayed for five days that felt like five years. Watching your child suffer and knowing you can't take the pain away is a kind of heartache that's impossible to describe. I prayed and pleaded with God in that hospital room. I tried to stay strong in front of him, but when the nurses left, and the lights dimmed, I go to the chapel and weep in silence. Not out of a lack of faith—but out of the weight of it all.

Still, somewhere between the hospital walls and my breaking point, **God was there**. He didn't always speak loudly, but I felt Him—in the calm during chaos, in the silent moments when my tears hit the floor and no one saw but Him. He was in the gaps. Filling the places where my strength failed.

Then came **2024**. A year that didn't just stretch me—it *emptied* me.

Once again, I was back and forth between hospitals. But this time, it wasn't just my mother, aunt or my biological dad. It was my Papa—my rock, my steady place—who was battling cancer. A strong man, weathered by life but never broken by it. He had been through so much—loss, hardship, the kind of struggles you don't always put into words. And through it all, he remained the pillar of our family. Until, slowly, that pillar began to lean.

Time slowed to a crawl. I watched the strongest man I had ever known begin to grow tired. He didn't say much—he never was one to complain. But one night in that hospital, something shifted. He looked at me with eyes that were no longer just strong—they were *tired*. And he whispered the words I'll never forget:

"Baby, I'm sick. Baby, I'm real sick."

He had never said that before. Not once. Not even when things were obviously wrong. And in that moment, my soul knew—we were close to goodbye.

On **August 27, 2024**, Papa passed away.

The grief was suffocating. I cried so hard I felt like my insides were splitting. But not in front of others. I kept smiling for them, kept planning the funeral, kept cooking, cleaning, and showing up. But on the inside, I was mourning *everything*. My Papa. My childhood. My anchor. My protector. The grief hit places I didn't even know existed.

Yet even in that valley—**God met me.**

"My grace is sufficient for you, for My strength is made perfect in weakness."
— *2 Corinthians 12:9*

It wasn't that He stopped the pain. But He *carried* me through it. He strengthened me in ways I didn't understand at the time. I look back now and realize—I was walking on water, and it was His hand holding me up.

But the storms didn't stop.

While still grieving my Papa, I started hearing whispers at work. The place I had dedicated **26 years** of my life to was preparing to shut down. My stability. My income. My daily rhythm. And before long, those whispers became headlines: *Our distribution center was officially closing on February 28, 2025.*

I hadn't even had time to grieve properly, and now I had to worry about how to keep the lights on. The bills didn't care that I was in mourning. The world kept spinning—and I had to spin with it.

Then my biological father's health took a turn. Once again, I found myself in hospital hallways—those all-too-familiar corridors of waiting, praying, and believing. My body was tired, my spirit worn, but I pressed on. At the same time, Auntie Mattie was back in a hospital bed too. I felt like I was caught in a loop I couldn't escape. The days ran together—early mornings, late nights, back and forth between rooms, trying to be present for everyone when I barely had anything left to give.

And then came the heartbreak I didn't think I could bear.

On **January 27, 2025**, just five months after laying my Papa to rest, I lost my **biological father** as well.

Two dads. Five months apart.

But my biological father was more than a man. **He was a legend**.

He walked in wisdom, carried himself with dignity, and spoke with the kind of authority that could only come from spending time in the presence of God. He wasn't just my father—**he was my example, my mentor, my earthly model of faith**. When he spoke, you listened. Not because he demanded it, but because there was *truth* in his words—biblical, life-tested truth.

He had the kind of faith that didn't waver under pressure. The kind of courage that stood tall even in sickness. He loved God passionately and served people wholeheartedly. His hands were strong, his prayers even stronger. He had a way of seeing people—not just their appearance, but their heart. He poured wisdom into everyone he encountered, and if you stood still long enough, you'd leave with a lesson that would shape your life.

To me, he was more than blood—**he was legacy**.

I carry his lessons with me daily. His unwavering faith. His quiet strength. His deep, unwavering love for God and for people. And now, though he is no longer physically with me, his spirit lives on in every decision I make, every scripture I speak, every moment I choose grace over grief.

Losing him broke something in me—but it also built something in me.

A deeper dependence on God.

A more intentional love for others.

And a renewed commitment to walk in the wisdom he modeled for me all my life.

How do you grieve two fathers, keep a household running, stay emotionally available to your children, and try to breathe under the weight of it all? The answer is: *you don't—not without God*.

I was stretched beyond comprehension. My prayers were groans. My faith was not loud—but it was *real*. I didn't always shout it from the rooftops, but I clung to it like a lifeline. And still—**God carried me.**

"I have fought the good fight, I have finished the race, I have kept the faith."
— *2 Timothy 4:7*

When the final blow came and I officially lost my job, I sat in my car and cried until my chest ached. No job. No Papa. No biological father. Just me—and God.

But even then—**my faith remained intact.**

I kept repeating what had become my anthem. A phrase that didn't just describe my pain—it defined my perseverance:

**"The stretch is real."**

It wasn't cute. It wasn't trendy. It was a truth forged in the fire of grief and uncertainty. The stretch was real—but so was my determination. So was my faith. So was my God.

Now, I walk in a season of complete dependence on Him. I have no earthly backup plan. No father figures to call. But I do have a Heavenly Father who has never missed a moment. Never failed to catch a tear. Never walked away when things got heavy.

**And I'm still standing.**

Not because I figured it out—but because **He never let me fall.**

And here's what I've learned:

**He didn't bring me this far to leave me now.**

After all the loss, the long nights, the prayers I couldn't even say out loud, I realized this truth: **the stretch doesn't end when you reach the top.**

Sometimes, it gets harder.

Because trusting God isn't just something you do in a crisis—it's something you *become*. It's a rhythm. A relationship. A declaration that says, *"Though He slay me, yet will I trust Him."*

This chapter of my life wasn't just about grief—it was about growth. It wasn't just about endings—it was about *encounters*. Encounters with a faithful God who fills in the gaps when life tears holes in your heart.

To every single mother who feels like she's breaking:
To every woman who's stretched beyond her limit:
To every soul who's lost more than she thought she could survive:

This chapter is for you.

Your stretch is not your end.

It's the setup for your *strength*.

And God? He's already in the gaps.

*The next stretch would teach me that trusting God is not a one-time decision—it's a lifetime journey.*

---

**Reflection Questions:**

1. Where in your life have you seen God fill in the gaps—financially, emotionally, spiritually?
2. Are you in a season where God is calling you to obey—even when it doesn't make sense?
3. What would it look like to trust Him completely, even in grief and uncertainty?


**Prayer:**
Father, You are my provider, my comforter, and my strength. Even when life stretches me beyond what I think I can bear, You remain faithful. Thank You for filling every gap, holding me in grief, and guiding me into new places with divine purpose. Help me to trust Your plan, even when the path feels uncertain. In Jesus' name, Amen.

## LESSONS FROM THE STRETCH

- God specializes in filling gaps that human effort cannot.
- Obedience often precedes understanding.
- Provision often looks small but carries divine impact.
- Every delay and detour can be preparation for deeper purpose.
- Grief doesn't disqualify your growth — it deepens it.

'My grace is
sufficient for you,
for my power is
made perfect in weakness.'
– 2 Corinthians 12.9

I have fought the good fight,
I have finished the race,
I have kept the faith.
– 2 Timothy 4:7

# Chapter Five: "Released to Rise"

## Divine Connections and Necessary Separations

Throughout my journey of stretching, I thank Jesus for allowing me to meet some true Kingdom seekers—those whose hearts beat in rhythm with Heaven. These divine connections came like water in dry places—refreshing, purposeful, and perfectly timed. They reminded me that while the stretch is personal, it's never meant to be isolated. God will place people on your path who are divinely assigned to help carry the weight of the next level.

In the same breath, I also thank Him for the relationships He *removed*. As painful as it was, I've learned that not all relationships are meant to last a lifetime. Some people were part of my *history*, not my *destiny*. And when God starts to shift you, He'll shift your surroundings, too.

"They went out from us, but they were not of us; for if they had been of us, they would have continued with us."
— *1 John 2:19 (ESV)*

God began to highlight connections that had become toxic, draining, or distracting. People I once leaned on began to fall silent. Some grew distant without explanation. Others left with words that stung. I cried. I questioned. I even tried to reach back. But in those moments, God whispered, "I'm making room for the right ones."

I had to trust that *He knows who belongs on the journey*. Not everyone can walk with you when God is birthing something new in you.

"Bad company corrupts good character."
— *1 Corinthians 15:33 (NIV)*

And then, almost unexpectedly, I began to meet Kingdom-minded individuals. Spirit-filled sisters and brothers who prayed over me, a mentor who poured into me, and divine encouragers who didn't just see my pain—they saw my promise. These weren't coincidences; they were *covenant connections*.

"As iron sharpens iron, so one person sharpens another."
— *Proverbs 27:17 (NIV)*

---

### ✧ *Mini-Stretch Testimony*

There was a time when I clung tightly to a friendship that had lasted over a decade. We had been through so much together—birthdays, funerals, and even our children's milestones. But as God began to stretch me, I noticed our conversations became shallow, even competitive. What once felt like comfort started to feel like compromise.

I remember fasting and asking God if I was imagining things. And then came the confirmation—a message that was not only hurtful but exposed a heart posture I hadn't wanted to see. That night, I wept. But I also *released*. And in the months that followed, God brought two new women into my life—sisters in Christ who didn't just pray *with* me, they prayed *for* me. Divine replacements. Divine timing.

## Life Application

- Evaluate your current connections. Are they feeding your faith or draining your purpose?
- Ask God for wisdom to discern who is assigned to your destiny and who has fulfilled their role.
- Be open to divine replacements. God never subtracts without planning a divine addition.

## Prayer of Release and Alignment

**Father God,**
Thank You for being intentional with every relationship in my life. Help me to release what no longer serves Your purpose for me and to embrace what You are sending next. Give me discernment to recognize Kingdom connections and courage to let go of those not aligned with where You're taking me. I trust You in the stretch—even in my relationships. Amen.

## Scripture Meditations

- **John 15:2** – "He cuts off every branch in me that bears no fruit…while every branch that does bear fruit he prunes so that it will be even more fruitful."
- **Amos 3:3** – "Can two walk together, unless they are agreed?"
- **Proverbs 13:20** – "Walk with the wise and become wise, for a companion of fools suffers harm."
- **Ecclesiastes 3:6** – "A time to search and a time to give up, a time to keep and a time to throw away."

# Chapter Six: The Stretch Doesn't End on the Mountain

*"Victory isn't the end of the stretch — it's the beginning of new strength."*

You would think that once you say "yes" to God, once you walk in your calling, once you start standing in obedience—things would finally settle.

But what I have come to know deep in my soul is this: **the stretch does not stop on the mountain. Sometimes, it is just the beginning.**

2024 taught me that life will not always pause for you to catch your breath. And just when I thought the storm had calmed, **2025 came with another wave**.

In **April 2025**, my **Babyboy had a diabetic relapse** that landed him in the hospital. Out of nowhere, his numbers spiked. I was watching him slip into exhaustion and struggle—and I felt completely helpless. I rushed him to **UAB** where he was hospitalized for **three days**. As a mother, that kind of fear hits differently. Watching your child hooked up to machines, waiting for updates, praying with everything you got—it changes you.

And I was still **unemployed**.
No insurance - It had just ended -March 31st. Little savings. Just faith.

I remember sitting by his bedside asking God, "How am I going to pay for all of this?"

But before the worry could turn into panic, God reminded me who He is.

When we left that hospital—**everything was paid in full.**
Every doctor visit.
Every prescription.
Every single cost.

**Paid. In. Full.**

**"And my God will supply all your needs according to His riches in glory in Christ Jesus." (Philippians 4:19)**

There it was again—proof in the stretch.

I did not know how, but God showed me He already had it handled. And He used that moment to remind me:
**The stretch is real. But God! God is more real.**

He did not just show up—He provided.

He did not just cover the hospital bill—He covered *me* with peace.

He did not just make a way—He made *the* way.

That moment shifted me. Because the truth is, I am still stretched. I am still between "God, I don't know how" and "But I know You will." I am still walking by faith, still waiting on doors to open, still listening for direction.

But here is what I know for sure:

**He did not bring me through everything I have survived just to let me fall now.**
He is still Jehovah Jireh.

He is still the Way Maker.
He is still the Lifter Of My Head.
And He is still God in every gap of my life.

But isn't it just like God to build something solid from something society calls shaky? The stretch did not stop when I got licensed in ministry.

It didn't stop when I got married. It didn't stop when I obeyed.
**Because stretching isn't punishment—it's God's process.**

It's how He builds us. Grows us. Prepares us. *Reveals Himself to us.*

What the world labeled a mistake, God saw as ministry in the making.

So today, I declare again—Bold and Unashamed:
**"THE STRETCH IS REAL. But my God is more real."**

So, if you are wondering whether the stretch will ever end, let me encourage you: the goal is not just surviving the stretch—it is becoming stronger, wiser, and closer to Him because of it.

*Before we close this journey, I have one more word of encouragement just for you...*

**Reflection Questions:**

1. Where in your life is God showing Himself as Provider right now—even if it's not how you expected?
2. What area of your faith has been most stretched recently?
3. Can you name a moment when you saw God pay what you could not, open what you could not, or heal what you couldn't?

**Prayer:**
Lord, You are my Source. You are my Provider. When I don't have enough, You remind me that You are more than enough. Thank You for showing up in my son's life, in my finances, and in every stretch of this journey. I trust You with the unknown because You've proven You're faithful in the unexpected. I will keep declaring Your name as I walk by faith. In Jesus' name, Amen.

## LESSONS FROM THE STRETCH

- The stretch continues even after breakthroughs.
- God's provision is not limited by our lack.
- Faith is trusting even when resources run out.
- God's realness is revealed in our most desperate moments.
- Stretching seasons are invitations to deeper intimacy with Him.

Now it's your turn to reflect.

God has been stretching you, too—and He's ready to meet you right where you are. Take a moment to journal your stretch journey before we conclude.

# Stretch Reflection Journal Section

Use the following pages to reflect on your own stretch journey. Write openly. Be honest. Let God meet you in the margins.

**1. What season of stretching am I currently in?**

_____
_____
_____

**2. What are some ways I've seen God provide or protect during this time?**

_____
_____
_____

**3. What old habits, people, or mindsets is God asking me to release in this stretch?**

_____
_____
_____

**4. What scriptures speak to me the most right now?**

_____
_____
_____

**5. What is God revealing to me about myself in this season?**

_____
_____
_____


**6. What has this book stirred in me that I need to surrender to God?**

_____
_____
_____

# Stretch Reflection Journal
# Additional Section

# Prayer Declaration:

Write your own "stretch" prayer here. Let it be your cry, your confession, and your commitment.

_____
_____
_____
_____
_____
_____
_____
_____
_____
_____
_____
_____
_____
_____
_____
_____
_____
_____
_____
_____

# Stretch Declarations

Speak these declarations boldly over your life. Let your faith rise even in the middle of the stretch!

---

I declare that God is stretching me, not to break me, but to build me.
I declare that every stretch is preparing me for greater purpose.
I declare that God's grace covers every area where I feel weak.
I declare that my past mistakes cannot disqualify my future victories.
I declare that I am more than a conqueror through Christ who strengthens me.
I declare that provision will meet me where my strength runs out.
I declare that I will not fear the stretch — I will embrace it.
I declare that beauty is rising from every place that once held ashes.
I declare that God's promises are yes and amen over my life.
I declare that even in the valley, God is leading me to the mountain.
I declare that the stretch is real, but my God is more real.
I declare that what God has started in me, He will surely complete.

Stretch me, Lord — because I know You are preparing me for more than I can see right now. I trust You with the process. I trust You with the promise. Amen.

# Scripture Meditation Page

**Write the scripture God is highlighting for you today:**
*(Example: Isaiah 40:29 — "He gives strength to the weary and increases the power of the weak.")*

_____
_____


**What is God speaking to me through this scripture?**
*(Write down personal reflections, insights, or encouragement.)*

_____
_____


**How can I apply this Word to my current stretch season?**
*(Practical steps, faith declarations, changes in thinking or living.)*

_____
_____


**Prayer Inspired by the Scripture:**
*(Write your personal prayer back to God based on what He showed you.)*

_____
_____

# Closing Word of Encouragement

## *"You Made It Through the Stretch"*

To every woman, mother, believer, or weary heart who has flipped through the pages of my journey—this is for you:

You are not alone in the stretch.

If life has pulled you, pressed you, and pushed you past your limits, I pray this book has reminded you that **God is present in every part of the process**. You don't have to be perfect to be called. You don't have to be fully healed to be useful. And you don't have to understand everything to trust that He is working it *all* for your good.

Stretching isn't just about pain. It's about **preparation**. It's about being expanded so God can pour more into you. It's about growing into the version of yourself that *only pressure could produce*.

So don't despise the stretch. Embrace it. Your stretch may not look like mine, but your victory will still glorify God.

Keep walking. Keep weeping if you must. Keep worshiping. Keep working the Word. And above all—keep trusting the One who started the good work in you. He's not done yet.

**The stretch is real, but God is more real.**
And if He's stretching you, He's also sustaining you. You're still standing—**because grace won't let you fall**

**Lord God,**

**Thank You for every stretch, every tear, and every triumph that brought us closer to You.**

**Thank You for being the God who never wastes our pain, but turns it into purpose.**

**I bless every reader who has walked through these pages with me. I declare that their stretching season will not break them — it will build them. I declare that every place that felt barren will bloom again, every weary heart will find renewed strength, and every broken place will be filled with Your unshakable grace.**

**May they rise from this journey stronger, wiser, and more anchored in Your love than ever before.**

**Let every stretch birth new faith, new dreams, and new doors of opportunity.**

Surround them with Your favor. Crown them with Your peace. Breathe fresh hope into their dry places. And remind them daily that the God who started the good work in them will be faithful to complete it.

I bless them to trust You in the stretching.
I bless them to find joy even in the waiting.
I bless them to walk boldly into the future You have prepared for them.

The stretch is real, but Your faithfulness is greater.

In the mighty, matchless, unchanging name of Jesus,
Amen.

Connect with the Author

The journey doesn't end here — it's just beginning!

I would love to stay connected with you as you continue your stretch journey, walk in your purpose, and experience God's faithfulness in new ways.

Join me for encouragement, ministry updates, devotionals, and community moments as we stretch together — and grow together — in Christ!

## Follow Melanie Lane:

**Instagram:**
@TheStretchCircle

**Facebook:**
@TheStretchCircle

**Ministry Group:**
**The Stretch Circle** — a Kingdom ministry focused on spiritual growth, healing, and living stretched but victorious!

✉ **Email:**
mlane@thestretchcircle.com

Thank you for being part of this stretch journey with me. I'm cheering you on, praying for your strength, and believing that the best is yet to come!
— **Melanie Lane**

### The Stretch is Real — But So Is the Victory. ™

**Melanie Lane** is a passionate minister, writer, speaker, and servant leader dedicated to helping others find hope, healing, and strength through their stretch seasons. With a heart rooted in compassion and a life anchored in faith, she empowers others to persevere through pain and rise through purpose.

A devoted mother of three and a woman after God's own heart, Melanie openly shares her powerful journey of navigating brokenness, disappointment, and profound loss—reminding readers that God does His deepest work in our most stretching moments. Through every valley and victory, Melanie remains a living testimony that **grace carries, healing is possible, and the stretch is never wasted**.

Through transparent storytelling and biblical truth, Melanie empowers readers to see that stretching is not punishment — it's preparation for purpose. She is the founder of *The Stretch Circle*, a new growing ministry focused on spiritual growth, restoration, and victorious living.

When she's not writing or ministering, Melanie loves spending time with her family, encouraging others, and reminding everyone she meets that **the stretch is real — but so is the victory**.

*God Bless You!*

Made in the USA
Columbia, SC
30 June 2025